5-6

Written by
Caryn Day

Editors: Jennifer Dashef and Alaska Hults
Illustrator: Donna Catanese
Cover Illustrator: Donna Catanese
Designers: Moonhee Pak and Marek/Janci Design
Cover Designer: Moonhee Pak
Art Director: Tom Cochrane
Project Director: Carolea Williams

Special thanks to all the teachers and children at Noble Elementary School for contributing mental math problem ideas:
Irene Budworth, Barbara Franke, Liliana Isaad, Yvonne Raphael, Sylvia White, Gayle Wolf, Alan Arjon, David Barrientos, Kevin Casteneda, Amy Chanbopha Sen, Paul Collins, Danny Garay, Anabel Gomez, Melray Green, Mario Guzman, Isabel Mendoza, Franklin Monjaras, Raul Ortiz, Andrew Perez, Kim Sandoval, Henry Segovia, and Janessa Suguitan.

Table of Contents

Introduction

Mental math involves the ability to quickly make mathematical calculations without the aid of a calculator, paper and pencil, or a computer. The problems in *Mental Math* provide daily opportunities for students to practice mental calculations as well as improve their math, listening, problem-solving, and communication skills. Students learn and store math facts and operations during each mental calculation and apply this knowledge to the solution of new problems.

Mental math problems are a great way to start your class's day. Use them to help students focus, listen, and warm up. Need to fill a few minutes in your daily schedule? The problems in *Mental Math* also make perfect "sponge" activities. Adapt the problems to meet your unique instructional needs and make them an essential component of your daily classroom schedule.

This resource features 110 mental math problems on reproducible cards; suggestions for using the problems for individual, small-group, and whole-group activities; assessment tips; and a reproducible record chart and game sheet. Designed to reinforce your whole-class lessons, the problems include the following content and process areas from the National Council of Teachers of Mathematics:

- number and operation
- patterns
- geometry
- data analysis
- problem solving
- reasoning and proof
- communication
- connections
- representation

Encourage students to think of the problems as having "friendly numbers"—numbers they can easily compute in their head—and you will create a learning environment where all students experience mental math success!

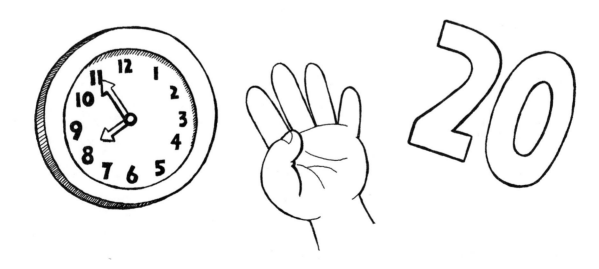

Getting Started

Introduce mental math problems at the beginning of the year. Use them to build on current math concepts. Start by photocopying and cutting apart the reproducible mental math cards. Read each problem in advance to make sure students are familiar with the math concept(s), skill(s), and interdisciplinary facts needed to correctly calculate the answer. Refer to page 6 for an explanation of the skills that relate to each math concept presented in this book. You may choose to present one or several mental math problems per day in the sequence that best meets the needs of your class. Modify individual problems to make them easier or more challenging, depending on the skill level of your students.

Read a mental math problem to the class. Give students ten seconds to calculate each step of the problem. (The answer for each step is listed in parentheses for quick reference.) If you find that some students are struggling with mental calculations, ask them to show their answer for each step (rather than just their final answer).

The problems in *Mental Math* direct students to whisper their answer to their neighbor or show it on their fingers. However, feel free to modify the directions to have students answer problems by showing the appropriate number card, writing on an individual chalkboard or dry erase board, or writing in a math journal.

Review the final answer to each problem by having a volunteer explain how he or she calculated each step. Ask the rest of the class to give a thumbs-up sign if they think a calculation is correct. Write correct calculations on the chalkboard for clarification or reinforcement. Show students the most effective way to group or break down numbers for problems. Have students compare and contrast different calculations to find the quickest way to get the correct answer.

Assessment

The best way to assess students' skill level and their comprehension of each problem is to carefully observe their reactions. Watch to see who hesitates and who quickly responds. Note students' reactions when they whisper answers to each other.

A math journal is another way to assess mental math ability. Staple several sheets of blank paper inside a construction paper cover to create a mental math journal for each student. Once a week, have students write in their journal their answers and an explanation of how they calculated each answer

(in place of having volunteers explain their calculations). Use the Record Chart (page 8) to keep track of individual progress. Review each student's journal, and write a check under the corresponding concept(s) for each problem the student answered correctly.

Use the math journals and the data from the record chart to determine if a student uses effective calculation methods. Present mini-lessons on specific math concepts to individual students or small groups.

Math Concepts

Mental math problems incorporate a variety of math concepts. The following list provides a definition of each concept and the ways in which it appears in this book. Use the parenthetical reference to locate where each concept first appears.

Addition: Find the total number of items when two groups of items are combined. Students solve one- to four-digit addition problems. (#1, page 10)

Calendar: Demonstrate knowledge of periods of time. (#1, page 10)

Decimals: Solve a problem with decimals. Students add, subtract, multiply, and divide decimals and determine the decimal equivalent of a fraction. (#47, page 33)

Division: Find the number of times a group contains a given subgroup. Students solve double- and triple-digit division problems and calculate square roots, percentages, and halves. (#4, page 11)

Fractions: Find a part of a whole. Students add and subtract fractions; determine the value of a fraction of a number; and determine the fractional equivalent of a decimal or percent. (#6, page 12)

Money: Demonstrate knowledge of the value of coins and dollars. (#4, page 11)

Multiplication: Calculate the total number of items consisting of equal groups. Students solve one- to four-digit multiplication problems; double, triple, and square numbers; multiply by ten and exponents of ten; and solve exponential problems. (#1, page 10)

Number Sequence: Identify the order or compare values of two numbers. (#7, page 13)

Place Value: Determine the value of a digit by its position within a number. (#3, page 11)

Rounding Numbers: Find the nearest whole number or given place value. (#2, page 10)

Shapes: Demonstrate knowledge of the properties of a named polygon. (#7, page 13)

Subtraction: Compare two groups and find the difference, or find what is left when one group is taken from another. Students solve one- to four-digit subtraction problems. (#4, page 11)

Time: Calculate time to the minute, quarter hour, half hour, and hour. (#20, page 19)

Vocabulary: Identify and use math vocabulary (e.g., prime, factor, mean) to solve problems. (#8, page 13)

Mental Math Extensions

There are so many fun ways to use *Mental Math.* The following individual, small-group, and whole-group activities feature a variety of ways to use the mental math cards.

• Give two students 14 mental math cards. Ask one student to shuffle and deal all of the cards. Have students alternate reading their cards to their partner. If their partner calculates the problem correctly, have the reader give that card to his or her partner. If their partner is incorrect, have the reader discard the card. Encourage students to try to collect more cards each time they repeat the game.

• Select a class set of mental math cards. Divide the class into two teams. Call one player from each team to the front of the class, and place a bell in front of each player. Read a mental math card. The first player to ring the bell and give the correct answer earns a point for his or her team. If the first player gives an incorrect answer, invite the other player to respond. Continue the game with two new players and a new mental math card until each student has had two turns. Applaud both teams when the last card has been played.

• Place 30 mental math cards at a learning center. Give each student at the center a Game Sheet (page 9) and pencil. Ask one student in the group to shuffle the cards and place them in a pile. Have students take turns reading a card while the remaining group members record the mental math card number in the *Card #* column and their answer in the

Answer column of their game sheet. Have the reader check the players' answers. Invite students to record one point in the *Points* column next to each correct answer. The student with the most points wins the game.

• Ask students to write their own mental math problems. Challenge students to write at least five steps in their problems. Review the problems for accuracy, and then share them with the class.

Record Chart

Mental Math Problems _____ to _____

Name	Shapes	Number Sequence	Calendar	Addition	Subtraction	Time	Money	Place Value	Rounding Numbers	Multiplication	Division	Fractions	Decimals	Vocabulary	Other:							

Mental Math • 5–6 © 2001 Creative Teaching Press

Game Sheet

Card #	Answer	Points	Card #	Answer	Points	Card #	Answer	Points

     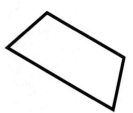

MENTAL MATH 1

Start with the number of days in one week. (7)

Double that number. (14)

Add the digits together. (5)

Add 4. (9)

Show me your answer with your fingers. (9)

Math Concepts: calendar, multiplication, addition

Mental Math • 5–6 © 2001 Creative Teaching Press

MENTAL MATH 2

Start with the number 9. (9)

Double that number. (18)

Add the digits together. (9)

Round that number to the nearest ten. (10)

Show me your answer with your fingers. (10)

Math Concepts: multiplication, addition, rounding numbers

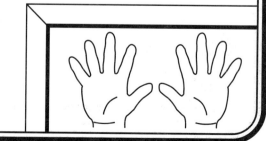

Mental Math • 5–6 © 2001 Creative Teaching Press

MENTAL MATH 3

Start with the number 12. (12)

Round that number to the nearest ten. (10)

Double that number. (20)

Multiply the digit in the ones place by the digit in the tens place. (0)

Whisper your answer to your neighbor. (0)

Math Concepts: rounding numbers, multiplication, place value

MENTAL MATH 4

Start with the number of days you are in school each week. (5)

Double that number. (10)

Subtract the number of pennies in one nickel. (5)

Divide that number by the number of nickels in one quarter (1)

Show me your answer with your fingers. (1)

Math Concepts: calendar, multiplication, subtraction, money, division

Mental Math • 5–6 © 2001 Creative Teaching Press

MENTAL MATH 5

Start with the number 12. (12)

Double that number. (24)

Add the digits together. (6)

Multiply that number by 3. (18)

Subtract the number of dimes in 80 cents. (10)

Show me your answer with your fingers. (10)

Math Concepts: multiplication, addition, subtraction, money

Mental Math • 5–6 © 2001 Creative Teaching Press

MENTAL MATH 6

Start with the number 32. (32)

Add the digits together. (5)

Add 1. (6)

Subtract $\frac{3}{4}$. ($5\frac{1}{4}$)

Whisper your answer to your neighbor. ($5\frac{1}{4}$)

Math Concepts: addition, subtraction, fractions

$$5\frac{1}{4}$$

Mental Math • 5–6 © 2001 Creative Teaching Press

MENTAL MATH 7

Start with the number of sides on a quadrilateral. (4)

Multiply that number by the number of planets in our solar system. (36)

Subtract the value of one dozen. (24)

Divide that number by the greater number: 4 or 6. (4)

Show me your answer with your fingers. (4)

Math Concepts: shapes, multiplication, subtraction, division, number sequence

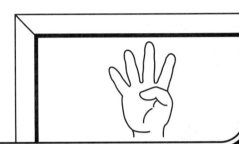

MENTAL MATH 8

Start with the number 32. (32)

Double that number. (64)

Divide that number by the numerator of $\frac{8}{10}$. (8)

Multiply that number by 10. (80)

Multiply the digit in the ones place by the digit in the tens place. (0)

Whisper your answer to your neighbor. (0)

Math Concepts: multiplication, division, vocabulary, fractions, place value

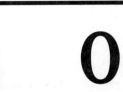

MENTAL MATH
9

Start with the number of days in April. (30)

Subtract the number of fingers and toes you have. (10)

Add the prime number: 2 or 4. (12)

Show me the digit in the ones place with your fingers. (2)

Math Concepts: calendar, subtraction, addition, vocabulary, place value

MENTAL MATH
10

Start with the number of years in one decade. (10)

Add the number of years in one century. (110)

Double that number. (220)

Add the digits together. (4)

Multiply that number by the number of sides on a triangle. (12)

Whisper your answer to your neighbor. (12)

Math Concepts: calendar, addition, multiplication, shapes

12

MENTAL MATH 11

Start with the number of days in one week. (7)

Subtract 5. (2)

Triple that number. (6)

Multiply that number by 7. (42)

Whisper your answer to your neighbor. (42)

Math Concepts: calendar, subtraction, multiplication

42

MENTAL MATH 12

Start with the lesser number: 105 or 501. (105)

Divide that number by 5. (21)

Multiply the digit in the ones place by the digit in the tens place. (2)

Show me your answer with your fingers. (2)

Math Concepts: number sequence, division, multiplication, place value

MENTAL MATH 13

Start with the number of years in one century. (100)

Divide that number by 2. (50)

Divide that number by 2. (25)

Add the digits together. (7)

Multiply that number by the denominator of $\frac{1}{3}$. (21)

Whisper your answer to your neighbor. (21)

Math Concepts: calendar, division, addition, multiplication, vocabulary, fractions

21

Mental Math • 5–6 © 2001 Creative Teaching Press

MENTAL MATH 14

Start with the number 300. (300)

Add three tens. (330)

Subtract five ones. (325)

Add the digits together. (10)

Show me your answer with your fingers. (10)

Math Concepts: addition, place value, subtraction

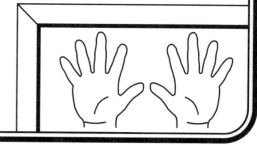

Mental Math • 5–6 © 2001 Creative Teaching Press

MENTAL MATH 15

Start with the value of ten tens. (100)

Subtract the number of pennies in one half-dollar. (50)

Divide that number by 2. (25)

Subtract the number of nickels in one quarter. (20)

Whisper your answer to your neighbor. (20)

Math Concepts: place value, subtraction, money, division

20

MENTAL MATH 16

Start with the number of days in June. (30)

Double that number. (60)

Triple that number. (180)

Subtract 100. (80)

Whisper your answer to your neighbor. (80)

Math Concepts: calendar, multiplication, subtraction

80

MENTAL MATH 17

Start with the number of years in two centuries. (200)

Multiply that number by 3. (600)

Divide that number by the number of hands you have. (300)

Find $\frac{1}{2}$ of that number. (150)

Whisper your answer to your neighbor. (150)

Math Concepts: calendar, multiplication, division, fractions

150

Mental Math • 5–6 © 2001 Creative Teaching Press

MENTAL MATH 18

Start with the number 20. (20)

Divide that number by the mean of 1, 2, and 3. (10)

Divide that number by the number of ears on a horse. (5)

Add the number of pennies in one quarter. (30)

Whisper your answer to your neighbor. (30)

Math Concepts: division, vocabulary, addition, money

30

Mental Math • 5–6 © 2001 Creative Teaching Press

MENTAL MATH 19

Start with the number 31. (31)

Subtract 1. (30)

Divide that number by the number of sides on a pentagon. (6)

Triple that number. (18)

Whisper your answer to your neighbor. (18)

Math Concepts: subtraction, division, shapes, multiplication

18

MENTAL MATH 20

Start with the number of seconds in one minute. (60)

Divide that number by the number of months in one year. (5)

Square that number. (25)

Multiply that number by 4. (100)

Divide that number by the number of pennies in one dollar. (1)

Show me your answer with your fingers. (1)

Math Concepts: time, division, calendar, multiplication, money

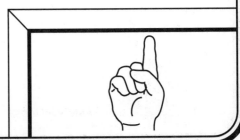

MENTAL MATH
21

Start with the number 80. (80)

Double that number. (160)

Subtract the number of minutes in half of an hour. (130)

Add the digits together. (4)

Show me your answer with your fingers. (4)

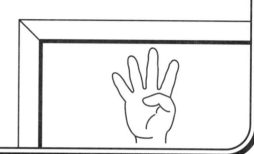

Math Concepts: multiplication, subtraction, time, addition

MENTAL MATH
22

Start with the greater number: 15 or 50. (50)

Divide that number by the number of fingers you have. (5)

Add the factor of 12: 3 or 5. (8)

Multiply that number by 4. (32)

Whisper your answer to your neighbor. (32)

Math Concepts: number sequence, division, addition, vocabulary, multiplication

32

MENTAL MATH

23

Start with the mean of 10, 12, and 14. (12)

Triple that number. (36)

Divide that number by the number of planets in our solar system. (4)

Double that number. (8)

Show me your answer with your fingers. (8)

Math Concepts: vocabulary, multiplication, division

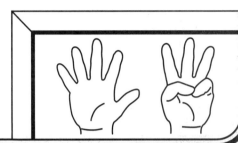

MENTAL MATH

24

Start with the multiple of 4: 10 or 12. (12)

Add the number of days in one week. (19)

Add the number of fingers and toes you have. (39)

Multiply the digit in the ones place by the digit in the tens place. (27)

Whisper your answer to your neighbor. (27)

Math Concepts: vocabulary, addition, calendar, multiplication, place value

27

Mental Math • 5–6 © 2001 Creative Teaching Press

MENTAL MATH 25

Start with the number 24. (24)

Double that number. (48)

Add 12. (60)

Divide that number by 2. (30)

Whisper your answer to your neighbor. (30)

Math Concepts: multiplication, addition, division

30

Mental Math • 5–6 © 2001 Creative Teaching Press

MENTAL MATH 26

Start with the number 32. (32)

Multiply the digit in the ones place by the digit in the tens place. (6)

Divide that number by 3. (2)

Add 8. (10)

Show me your answer with your fingers. (10)

Math Concepts: multiplication, place value, division, addition

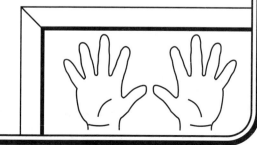

Mental Math • 5–6 © 2001 Creative Teaching Press

MENTAL MATH
27

Start with the range of 2, 6, and 10. (8)

Multiply that number by the number of parallel sides on a trapezoid. (16)

Add the number of pennies in one dime. (26)

Double that number. (52)

Whisper your answer to your neighbor. (52)

Math Concepts: vocabulary, multiplication, shapes, addition, money

52

MENTAL MATH
28

Start with the number of pennies in one dime. (10)

Divide that number by the number of feet you have. (5)

Multiply that number by 7. (35)

Add the digits together. (8)

Show me your answer with your fingers. (8)

Math Concepts: money, division, multiplication, addition

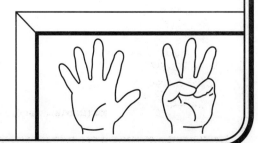

MENTAL MATH
29

Start with the absolute value of −9. (9)

Double that number. (18)

Add the digits together. (9)

Find $\frac{1}{3}$ of that number. (3)

Show me your answer with your fingers. (3)

Math Concepts: vocabulary, multiplication, addition, fractions

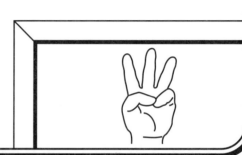

MENTAL MATH
30

Start with the number of days in November. (30)

Halve that number. (15)

Double that number. (30)

Multiply that number by 8. (240)

Whisper your answer to your neighbor. (240)

Math Concepts: calendar, division, multiplication

240

MENTAL MATH 31

Start with the number 16. (16)

Round that number to the nearest ten. (20)

Divide that number by 2. (10)

Triple that number. (30)

Whisper the digit in the ones place to your neighbor. (0)

Math Concepts: rounding numbers, division, multiplication, place value

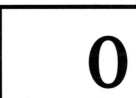

Mental Math • 5-6 © 2001 Creative Teaching Press

MENTAL MATH 32

Start with the number of days you are in school each week. (5)

Triple that number. (15)

Add the number of pennies in one half-dollar. (65)

Show me the digit in the tens place with your fingers. (6)

Math Concepts: calendar, multiplication, addition, money, place value

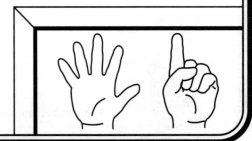

Mental Math • 5-6 © 2001 Creative Teaching Press

MENTAL MATH
33

Start with the number of minutes in a quarter of an hour. (15)

Divide that number by the number of sides on a triangle. (5)

Multiply that number by the number of sides on a rectangle. (20)

Double that number. (40)

Whisper your answer to your neighbor. (40)

Math Concepts: time, division, shapes, multiplication

40

MENTAL MATH
34

Start with the number 50. (50)

Add the number of pennies in one quarter. (75)

Subtract the number of sides on a pentagon. (70)

Divide that number by the number of dimes in one dollar. (7)

Show me your answer with your fingers. (7)

Math Concepts: addition, money, subtraction, shapes, division

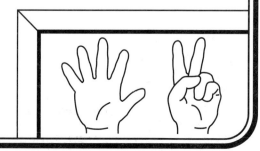

MENTAL MATH
35

Start with the value of 10^2. (100)

Double that number. (200)

Find $\frac{1}{5}$ of that number. (40)

Divide that number by 8. (5)

Show me your answer with your fingers. (5)

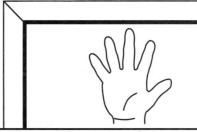

Math Concepts: multiplication, fractions, division

Mental Math • 5–6 © 2001 Creative Teaching Press

MENTAL MATH
36

Start with the number of days in June. (30)

Multiply that number by the number of hands you have. (60)

Add the number of sides on a pentagon. (65)

Add 7. (72)

Whisper your answer to your neighbor. (72)

Math Concepts: calendar, multiplication, addition, shapes

72

Mental Math • 5–6 © 2001 Creative Teaching Press

MENTAL MATH
37

Start with the number of eyes you have. (2)

Add the value of two dozen. (26)

Subtract the number of sides on a triangle. (23)

Add the digits together. (5)

Show me your answer with your fingers. (5)

Math Concepts: addition, subtraction, shapes

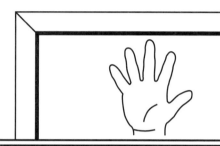

Mental Math • 5–6 © 2001 Creative Teaching Press

MENTAL MATH
38

Start with the number of socks in one pair. (2)

Triple that number. (6)

Add the number of sides on an octagon. (14)

Subtract 3. (11)

Whisper your answer to your neighbor. (11)

Math Concepts: multiplication, addition, shapes, subtraction

11

Mental Math • 5–6 © 2001 Creative Teaching Press

MENTAL MATH 39

Start with the number 312. (312)

Divide that number by 3. (104)

Add the digits together. (5)

Subtract $\frac{1}{8}$. ($4\frac{7}{8}$)

Whisper your answer to your neighbor. ($4\frac{7}{8}$)

Math Concepts: division, addition, subtraction, fractions

$$4\frac{7}{8}$$

Mental Math • 5–6 © 2001 Creative Teaching Press

MENTAL MATH 40

Start with the number of sides on an octagon. (8)

Multiply that number by the number of sides on a quadrilateral. (32)

Add the number of sides on a stop sign. (40)

Subtract half of that number. (20)

Whisper your answer to your neighbor. (20)

Math Concepts: shapes, multiplication, addition, subtraction, fractions

20

Mental Math • 5–6 © 2001 Creative Teaching Press

MENTAL MATH 41

Start with the number of pennies in one half-dollar. (50)

Add the number of sides on a hexagon. (56)

Multiply the digit in the ones place by the digit in the tens place. (30)

Subtract the value of two dozen. (6)

Show me your answer with your fingers. (6)

Math Concepts: money, addition, shapes, multiplication, place value, subtraction

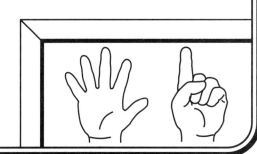

MENTAL MATH 42

Start with the number 32. (32)

Add the number of sides on a rhombus. (36)

Find $\frac{1}{6}$ of that number. (6)

Divide that number by the number of hands you have. (3)

Show me your answer with your fingers. (3)

Math Concepts: addition, shapes, fractions, division

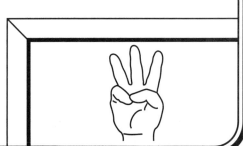

MENTAL MATH 43

Start with the number of months in one year. (12)

Subtract the number of sides on a parallelogram. (8)

Multiply that number by the number of angles in a triangle. (24)

Add the number of sides on a pentagon. (29)

Whisper your answer to your neighbor. (29)

Math Concepts: calendar, subtraction, shapes, multiplication, addition

29

MENTAL MATH 44

Start with the number of sides on a heptagon. (7)

Subtract 6. (1)

Multiply that number by 1,000. (1,000)

Divide that number by the number of nickels in 50 cents. (100)

Whisper your answer to your neighbor. (100)

Math Concepts: shapes, subtraction, multiplication, division, money

100

MENTAL MATH 45

Start with the number 7. (7)

Multiply that number by the number of ears you have. (14)

Divide that number by the number of moons Earth has. (14)

Find $\frac{1}{7}$ of that number. (2)

Show me your answer with your fingers. (2)

Math Concepts: multiplication, division, fractions

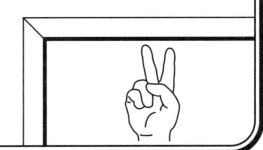

Mental Math • 5–6 © 2001 Creative Teaching Press

MENTAL MATH 46

Start with the number of quarters in one dollar. (4)

Multiply that number by 4. (16)

Subtract the number of wheels on a bicycle. (14)

Add the digits together. (5)

Show me your answer with your fingers. (5)

Math Concepts: money, multiplication, subtraction, addition

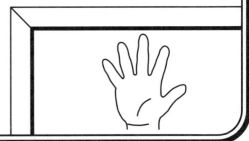

Mental Math • 5–6 © 2001 Creative Teaching Press

MENTAL MATH 47

Start with the number 28. (28)

Divide that number by the number of legs on a chair. (7)

Double that number. (14)

Divide that number by the number of arms you have. (7)

Add 0.3 to that number. (7.3)

Whisper your answer to your neighbor. (7.3)

Math Concepts: division, multiplication, addition, decimals

7.3

Mental Math • 5–6 © 2001 Creative Teaching Press

MENTAL MATH 48

Start with the value of one dozen. (12)

Double that number. (24)

Divide that number by 6. (4)

Subtract 0.5 from that number. (3.5)

Multiply that number by 1. (3.5)

Whisper your answer to your neighbor. (3.5)

Math Concepts: multiplication, division, subtraction, decimals

3.5

Mental Math • 5–6 © 2001 Creative Teaching Press

MENTAL MATH

49

Start with the number that represents July. (7)

Multiply that number by the number of sides on a square. (28)

Add 2. (30)

Think of the digit in the tens place. (3)

Subtract 0.7 from that number. (2.3)

Whisper your answer to your neighbor. (2.3)

Math Concepts: calendar, multiplication, shapes, addition, place value, subtraction, decimals

2.3

Mental Math • 5–6 © 2001 Creative Teaching Press

MENTAL MATH

50

Start with the number of pennies in one dime and one nickel. (15)

Subtract 3. (12)

Add the number of hours in half of one day. (24)

Divide that number by the number of angles in a hexagon. (4)

Show me your answer with your fingers. (4)

Math Concepts: money, subtraction, addition, time, division, shapes

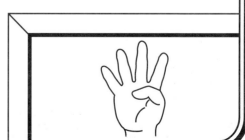

Mental Math • 5–6 © 2001 Creative Teaching Press

MENTAL MATH 51

Start with the time 3:30 p.m. (3:30 p.m.)

Add eleven hours. (2:30 a.m.)

Think of the number that represents the hour. (2)

Add the number of days in two weeks. (16)

Add the digits together. (7)

Show me your answer with your fingers. (7)

Math Concepts: time, addition, calendar

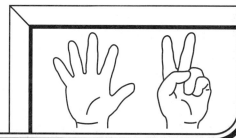

MENTAL MATH 52

Start with the number of days you are in school each week. (5)

Add 13. (18)

Subtract 0.6 from that number. (17.4)

Round that number to the nearest ten. (20)

Subtract 7. (13)

Whisper your answer to your neighbor. (13)

Math Concepts: calendar, addition, subtraction, decimals, rounding numbers

Mental Math • 5–6 © 2001 Creative Teaching Press

MENTAL MATH 53

Start with the fraction $\frac{5}{8}$. $\left(\frac{5}{8}\right)$

Add $\frac{4}{8}$. $\left(\frac{9}{8}\right)$

Add $\frac{4}{8}$. $\left(\frac{13}{8}\right)$

Multiply the numerator by 4. (52)

Whisper your answer to your neighbor. (52)

Math Concepts: fractions, addition, multiplication, vocabulary

52

MENTAL MATH 54

Start with the time 7:15 a.m. (7:15 a.m.)

Subtract 15 minutes. (7:00 a.m.)

Add one hour. (8:00 a.m.)

Think of the number that represents the hour. (8)

Add 15. (23)

Whisper your answer to your neighbor. (23)

Math Concepts: time, subtraction, addition

23

MENTAL MATH 55

Start with the number 13. (13)

Add the value of one dozen. (25)

Find $\frac{1}{5}$ of that number. (5)

Add the number of pennies in one nickel. (10)

Show me the digit in the tens place with your fingers. (1)

Math Concepts: addition, fractions, money, place value

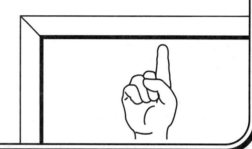

Mental Math • 5–6 © 2001 Creative Teaching Press

MENTAL MATH 56

Start with the number 206. (206)

Divide that number by the number of ankles you have. (103)

Add the digits together. (4)

Multiply that number by 2. (8)

Round that number to the nearest ten. (10)

Show me your answer with your fingers. (10)

Math Concepts: division, addition, multiplication, rounding numbers

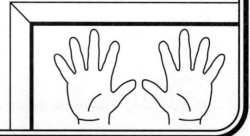

Mental Math • 5–6 © 2001 Creative Teaching Press

MENTAL MATH 57

Start with the number of days in January. (31)

Add 5. (36)

Divide that number by 3^2. (4)

Triple that number. (12)

Subtract $\frac{2}{3}$. ($11\frac{1}{3}$)

Whisper your answer to your neighbor. ($11\frac{1}{3}$)

Math Concepts: calendar, addition, division, multiplication, subtraction, fractions

$$11\frac{1}{3}$$

Mental Math • 5–6 © 2001 Creative Teaching Press

MENTAL MATH 58

Start with the number of minutes in one hour. (60)

Add two tens. (80)

Divide that number by the number of sides on a stop sign. (10)

Add the digits together. (1)

Show me your answer with your fingers. (1)

Math Concepts: time, addition, place value, division, shapes

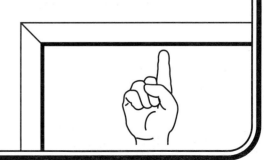

Mental Math • 5–6 © 2001 Creative Teaching Press

MENTAL MATH 59

Start with the number of months in one year. (12)

Double that number. (24)

Add the digits together. (6)

Square that number. (36)

Show me the digit in the ones place with your fingers. (6)

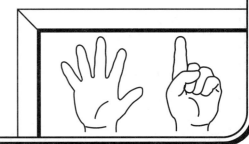

Math Concepts: calendar, multiplication, addition, place value

---

MENTAL MATH 60

Start with the factor of 20: 10 or 12. (10)

Add the number of pennies in one dime. (20)

Find $\frac{1}{4}$ of that number. (5)

Triple that number. (15)

Add the digits together. (6)

Show me your answer with your fingers. (6)

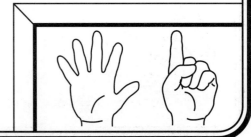

Math Concepts: vocabulary, addition, money, fractions, multiplication

MENTAL MATH 61

Start with the number of syllables in the word *cookie*. (2)

Multiply that number by the number of pennies in one nickel. (10)

Add 11. (21)

Add your favorite number. (answers will vary)

Multiply that number by 0. (0)

Whisper your answer to your neighbor. (0)

Math Concepts: multiplication, money, addition

0

MENTAL MATH 62

Start with the value of 5^2. (25)

Subtract 7. (18)

Multiply the digit in the ones place by the digit in the tens place. (8)

Double that number. (16)

Show me the digit in the ones place with your fingers. (6)

Math Concepts: multiplication, subtraction, place value

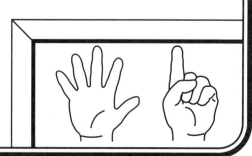

MENTAL MATH 63

Start with the time 4:55 p.m. (4:55 p.m.)

Subtract two hours. (2:55 p.m.)

Add ten minutes. (3:05 p.m.)

Round that time to the nearest hour. (3:00 p.m.)

Show me the hour with your fingers. (3)

Math Concepts: time, subtraction, addition, rounding numbers

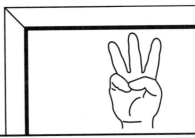

Mental Math • 5–6 © 2001 Creative Teaching Press

MENTAL MATH 64

Start with the value of one dozen. (12)

Subtract the number of toes you have. (2)

Multiply that number by the number of sides on an octagon. (16)

Add the digits together. (7)

Add 0.09 to that number. (7.09)

Whisper your answer to your neighbor. (7.09)

Math Concepts: subtraction, multiplication, shapes, addition, decimals

7.09

Mental Math • 5–6 © 2001 Creative Teaching Press

MENTAL MATH
65

Start with the value of one dollar. ($1.00)

Subtract the value of five pennies. (95¢)

Add the value of six dollars. ($6.95)

Round that value to the nearest dollar. ($7.00)

Add the value of 50 cents. ($7.50)

Whisper your answer to your neighbor. ($7.50)

Math Concepts: money, subtraction, addition, rounding numbers

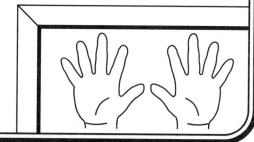

$7.50

Mental Math • 5–6 © 2001 Creative Teaching Press

MENTAL MATH
66

Start with the number 24. (24)

Add the number of angles in a triangle. (27)

Multiply the digit in the ones place by the digit in the tens place. (14)

Subtract 0.2 from that number. (13.8)

Round that number to the nearest ten. (10)

Show me your answer with your fingers. (10)

Math Concepts: addition, shapes, multiplication, place value, subtraction, decimals, rounding numbers

Mental Math • 5–6 © 2001 Creative Teaching Press

MENTAL MATH
67

Start with the number of days you are in school each week. (5)

Add $\frac{3}{4}$. $(5\frac{3}{4})$

Round that number to the nearest ten. (10)

Add the number of pennies in three nickels. (25)

Add the digits together. (7)

Show me your answer with your fingers. (7)

Math Concepts: calendar, addition, fractions, rounding numbers, money

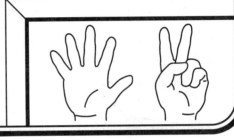

Mental Math • 5–6 © 2001 Creative Teaching Press

MENTAL MATH
68

Start with the number of years in one decade. (10)

Double that number. (20)

Add the number of dimes in three dollars. (50)

Multiply that number by 2. (100)

Multiply the digit in the ones place by the digit in the hundreds place. (0)

Whisper your answer to your neighbor. (0)

Math Concepts: calendar, multiplication, addition, money, place value

Mental Math • 5–6 © 2001 Creative Teaching Press

MENTAL MATH 69

Start with the number of days in one week. (7)

Add the number of fingers you have. (17)

Subtract 2. (15)

Divide that number by the number of vertices on a triangle. (5)

Add $\frac{5}{7}$. $(5\frac{5}{7})$

Whisper your answer to your neighbor. $(5\frac{5}{7})$

Math Concepts: calendar, addition, subtraction, division, shapes, fractions

$$5\frac{5}{7}$$

Mental Math • 5–6 © 2001 Creative Teaching Press

MENTAL MATH 70

Start with the time 7:00 p.m. (7:00 p.m.)

Add 45 minutes. (7:45 p.m.)

Subtract three hours. (4:45 p.m.)

Round that time to the nearest hour. (5:00 p.m.)

Whisper the time to your neighbor. (5:00 p.m.)

Math Concepts: time, addition, subtraction, rounding numbers

5:00

Mental Math • 5–6 © 2001 Creative Teaching Press

MENTAL MATH 71

Start with the number 12. (12)

Multiply that number by 10. (120)

Round that number to the nearest hundred. (100)

Double that number. (200)

Double that number. (400)

Show me the digit in the hundreds place with your fingers. (4)

Math Concepts: multiplication, rounding numbers, place value

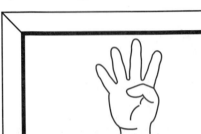

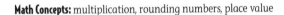

MENTAL MATH 72

Start with the greater decimal: 0.2 or 0.02. (0.2)

Add 0.06 to that number. (0.26)

Round that number to the nearest tenth. (0.3)

Double that number. (0.6)

Whisper your answer to your neighbor. (0.6)

Math Concepts: number sequence, decimals, addition, rounding numbers, multiplication

0.6

MENTAL MATH 73

Start with the value of 3^2. (9)

Multiply that number by the factor of 25: 7 or 5. (45)

Round that number to the nearest ten. (50)

Add 20. (70)

Show me the digit in the tens place with your fingers. (7)

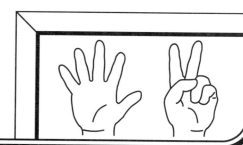

Math Concepts: multiplication, vocabulary, rounding numbers, addition, place value

Mental Math • 5–6 © 2001 Creative Teaching Press

MENTAL MATH 74

Start with the value of 10^3. (1,000)

Divide that number by 5. (200)

Add the digits together. (2)

Multiply that number by 10. (20)

Whisper your answer to your neighbor. (20)

Math Concepts: multiplication, division, addition

20

Mental Math • 5–6 © 2001 Creative Teaching Press

MENTAL MATH 75

Start with the number 100. (100)

Find 50% of that number. (50)

Add 5. (55)

Round that number to the nearest ten. (60)

Find $\frac{1}{6}$ of that number. (10)

Show me your answer with your fingers. (10)

Math Concepts: division, addition, rounding numbers, fractions

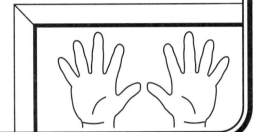

MENTAL MATH 76

Start with the fractional equivalent of 25%. ($\frac{1}{4}$)

Add $\frac{2}{4}$. ($\frac{3}{4}$)

Double that number. ($\frac{6}{4}$)

Think of that number as a mixed number. ($1\frac{1}{2}$)

Round that number to the nearest whole number. (2)

Show me your answer with your fingers. (2)

Math Concepts: fractions, addition, multiplication, rounding numbers

MENTAL MATH
77

Start with the lesser number: 0.5 or 5. (0.5)

Add 1.1 to that number. (1.6)

Divide that number by the number of wheels on a car. (0.4)

Multiply that number by 10^2. (40)

Whisper your answer to your neighbor. (40)

Math Concepts: number sequence, decimals, addition, division, multiplication

40

MENTAL MATH
78

Start with the composite number: 13 or 15. (15)

Add 35. (50)

Think of the fraction that number is of 100. ($\frac{1}{2}$)

Double that number. (1)

Show me your answer with your fingers. (1)

Math Concepts: vocabulary, addition, fractions, multiplication

MENTAL MATH
79

Start with the number that represents October. (10)

Multiply that number by 4^2. (160)

Round that number to the nearest hundred. (200)

Find $\frac{1}{4}$ of that number. (50)

Show me the digit in the tens place with your fingers. (5)

Math Concepts: calendar, multiplication, rounding numbers, fractions, place value

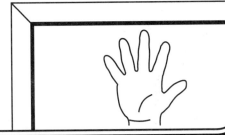

Mental Math • 5–6 © 2001 Creative Teaching Press

MENTAL MATH
80

Start with the fractional equivalent of 50%. ($\frac{1}{2}$)

Subtract $\frac{1}{4}$. ($\frac{1}{4}$)

Add the absolute value of −3. ($3\frac{1}{4}$)

Double that number. ($6\frac{1}{2}$)

Think of the decimal equivalent of that number. (6.5)

Round that number to the nearest whole number. (7)

Show me your answer with your fingers. (7)

Math Concepts: fractions, subtraction, addition, vocabulary, multiplication, decimals, rounding numbers

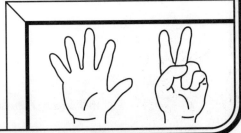

Mental Math • 5–6 © 2001 Creative Teaching Press

MENTAL MATH
81

Start with the greater value: six quarters or twelve dimes. ($1.50)

Add the value of one nickel. ($1.55)

Subtract the value of 50 pennies. ($1.05)

Subtract the value of 25 pennies. (80¢)

Whisper your answer to your neighbor. (80¢)

Math Concepts: money, addition, subtraction

80¢

MENTAL MATH
82

Start with the value of 10^4. (10,000)

Divide that number by 10^2. (100)

Find the square root of that number. (10)

Multiply that number by 3^2. (90)

Show me the digit in the tens place with your fingers. (9)

Math Concepts: multiplication, division, place value

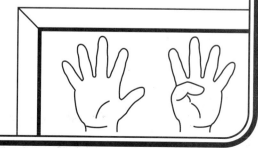

MENTAL MATH 83

Start with the time equivalent of noon. (12:00 p.m.)

Add four hours and 30 minutes. (4:30 p.m.)

Subtract 15 minutes. (4:15 p.m.)

Round that time to the nearest hour. (4:00 p.m.)

Whisper the time to your neighbor. (4:00 p.m.)

Math Concepts: time, addition, subtraction, rounding numbers

4:00

MENTAL MATH 84

Start with the number of sides on a heptagon. (7)

Add the number of sides on a decagon. (17)

Round that number to the nearest ten. (20)

Multiply that number by 10^2. (2,000)

Whisper your answer to your neighbor. (2,000)

Math Concepts: shapes, addition, rounding numbers, multiplication

2,000

MENTAL MATH

85

Start with the fractional equivalent of 75%. $(\frac{3}{4})$

Add the fractional equivalent of 25%. (1)

Add 0.8 to that number. (1.8)

Find $\frac{1}{2}$ of that number. (0.9)

Multiply that number by 3. (2.7)

Whisper your answer to your neighbor. (2.7)

Math Concepts: fractions, addition, decimals, multiplication

2.7

Mental Math • 5–6 © 2001 Creative Teaching Press

MENTAL MATH

86

Start with the average of 5, 8, and 8. (7)

Add the greater number: 0.5 or 0.05. (7.5)

Round that number to the nearest whole number. (8)

Multiply that number by 9. (72)

Show me the digit in the tens place with your fingers. (7)

Math Concepts: vocabulary, addition, number sequence, decimals, rounding numbers, multiplication, place value

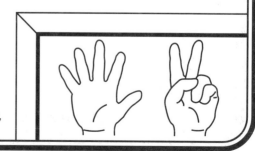

Mental Math • 5–6 © 2001 Creative Teaching Press

MENTAL MATH
87

Start with the numerator of $\frac{9}{12}$. (9)

Multiply that number by 2^3. (72)

Subtract 8. (64)

Find the square root of that number. (8)

Show me your answer with your fingers. (8)

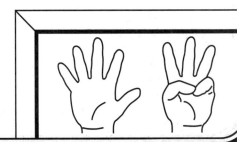

Math Concepts: vocabulary, fractions, multiplication, subtraction, division

MENTAL MATH
88

Start with the absolute value of 25. (25)

Find the square root of that number. (5)

Multiply that number by 3^2. (45)

Round that number to the nearest ten. (50)

Multiply the digit in the ones place by the digit in the tens place. (0)

Whisper your answer to your neighbor. (0)

Math Concepts: vocabulary, division, multiplication, rounding numbers, place value

MENTAL MATH
89

Start with the greater number: 2,020; 2,220; or 2,200. (2,220)

Subtract 200. (2,020)

Multiply the digit in the hundreds place by the digit in the thousands place. (0)

Add 0.7 to that number. (0.7)

Round that number to the nearest whole number. (1)

Show me your answer with your fingers. (1)

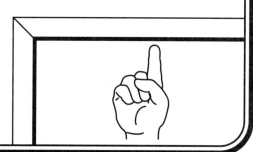

Math Concepts: number sequence, subtraction, multiplication, place value, addition, decimals, rounding numbers

Mental Math • 5–6 © 2001 Creative Teaching Press

MENTAL MATH
90

Start with the number of angles in a parallelogram. (4)

Multiply that number by the number of days in January. (124)

Add the digits together. (7)

Multiply that number by the prime number: 4, 5, or 6. (35)

Round that number to the nearest ten. (40)

Whisper your answer to your neighbor. (40)

Math Concepts: shapes, multiplication, calendar, addition, vocabulary, rounding numbers

40

Mental Math • 5–6 © 2001 Creative Teaching Press

MENTAL MATH 91

Start with the value of 7^2. (49)

Add the number of days in March. (80)

Subtract 2^3. (72)

Divide that number by 8. (9)

Find the square root of that number. (3)

Show me your answer with your fingers. (3)

Math Concepts: multiplication, addition, calander, subtraction, division

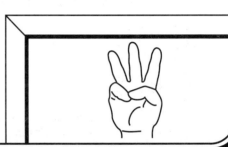

MENTAL MATH 92

Start with the multiple of 8: 22, 48, or 18. (48)

Round that number to the nearest ten. (50)

Subtract 14. (36)

Find the square root of that number. (6)

Show me your answer with your fingers. (6)

Math Concepts: vocabulary, rounding numbers, subtraction, division

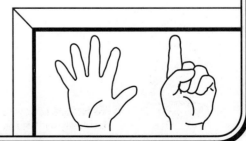

MENTAL MATH
93

Start with the number of pennies in one dollar. (100)

Add the multiple of 5: 94, 95, or 96. (195)

Round that number to the nearest hundred. (200)

Divide that number by 2. (100)

Find the square root of that number. (10)

Show me your answer with your fingers. (10)

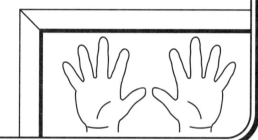

Math Concepts: money, addition, vocabulary, rounding numbers, division

MENTAL MATH
94

Start with the mode of 5, 7, 7, and 2. (7)

Add the value of one dozen. (19)

Subtract 0.7 from that number. (18.3)

Think of the digit in the ones place. (8)

Square that number. (64)

Whisper your answer to your neighbor. (64)

Math Concepts: vocabulary, addition, subtraction, decimals, place value, multiplication

64

MENTAL MATH 95

Start with the number 28. (28)

Add 10^3. (1,028)

Multiply the digit in the ones place by the digit in the tens place. (16)

Find the square root of that number. (4)

Add the number of years in two centuries. (204)

Whisper your answer to your neighbor. (204)

Math Concepts: addition, multiplication, place value, division, calendar

204

MENTAL MATH 96

Start with the number of years in one century. (100)

Find the square root of that number. (10)

Multiply that number by the composite number: 2, 13, or 8. (80)

Find $\frac{1}{4}$ of that number. (20)

Add 25. (45)

Round that number to the nearest ten. (50)

Whisper your answer to your neighbor. (50)

Math Concepts: calendar, division, multiplication, vocabulary, fractions, addition, rounding numbers

50

MENTAL MATH 97

Start with the number of pennies in one half-dollar. (50)

Add the radius of a circle with a diameter of 10. (55)

Round that number to the nearest ten. (60)

Add the denominator of $\frac{9}{15}$. (75)

Find the number of quarters equal to the value of that number. (3)

Show me your answer with your fingers. (3)

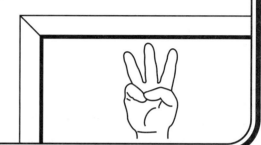

Math Concepts: money, addition, shapes, rounding numbers, vocabulary, fractions

Mental Math • 5–6 © 2001 Creative Teaching Press

MENTAL MATH 98

Start with the greater fraction: $\frac{5}{8}$ or $\frac{1}{2}$. ($\frac{5}{8}$)

Think of the denominator. (8)

Multiply that number by 10^3. (8,000)

Add the number of years in five centuries. (8,500)

Add the digits together. (13)

Round that number to the nearest ten. (10)

Show me the digit in the tens place with your fingers. (1)

Math Concepts: number sequence, fractions, vocabulary, multiplication, addition, calendar, rounding numbers, place value

Mental Math • 5–6 © 2001 Creative Teaching Press

MENTAL MATH
99

Mental Math • 5–6 © 2001 Creative Teaching Press

Start with the number of angles in a decagon. (10)

Square that number. (100)

Subtract 2^3. (92)

Subtract 11. (81)

Find the square root of that number. (9)

Show me your answer with your fingers. (9)

Math Concepts: shapes, multiplication, subtraction, division

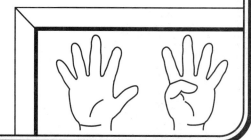

MENTAL MATH
100

Mental Math • 5–6 © 2001 Creative Teaching Press

Start with the number of days in October. (31)

Multiply that number by 10. (310)

Add the square root of 25. (315)

Multiply the digit in the ones place by the digit in the tens place by the digit in the hundreds place. (15)

Round that number to the nearest ten. (20)

Whisper your answer to your neighbor. (20)

Math Concepts: calendar, multiplication, addition, division, place value, rounding numbers

20

MENTAL MATH 101

Start with the prime number: 21, 12, or 2. (2)

Multiply that number by 5^2. (50)

Add the greater number: 0.7 or 0.07. (50.7)

Subtract 10.3 from that number. (40.4)

Divide that number by 2. (20.2)

Whisper your answer to your neighbor. (20.2)

Math Concepts: vocabulary, multiplication, addition, number sequence, decimals, subtraction, division

20.2

MENTAL MATH 102

Start with the value of two quarters and five pennies. (55¢)

Double that value. ($1.10)

Round that value to the nearest dollar. ($1.00)

Find the number of nickels in that value. (20)

Show me the digit in the tens place with your fingers. (2)

Math Concepts: money, multiplication, rounding numbers, place value

MENTAL MATH 103

Start with the number of hours in one day. (24)

Double that number. (48)

Divide that number by 10. (4.8)

Round that number to the nearest whole number. (5)

Show me your answer with your fingers. (5)

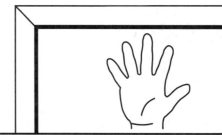

Math Concepts: time, multiplication, division, decimals, rounding numbers

Mental Math • 5–6 © 2001 Creative Teaching Press

MENTAL MATH 104

Start with the number of pennies in one nickel. (5)

Multiply that number by the composite number: 2, 5, or 9. (45)

Double that number. (90)

Think of the digit in the tens place. (9)

Show me the square root of that number with your fingers. (3)

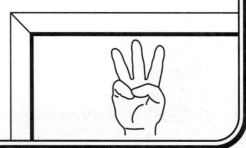

Math Concepts: money, multiplication, vocabulary, place value, division

Mental Math • 5–6 © 2001 Creative Teaching Press

MENTAL MATH 105

Start with the number of days in December. (31)

Add the multiple of 7: 42, 44, or 46. (73)

Multiply the digit in the ones place by the digit in the tens place. (21)

Round that number to the nearest ten. (20)

Show me the digit in the tens place with your fingers. (2)

Math Concepts: calendar, addition, vocabulary, multiplication, place value, rounding numbers

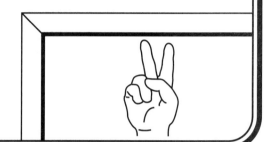

Mental Math • 5–6 © 2001 Creative Teaching Press

MENTAL MATH 106

Start with the number 212. (212)

Divide that number by the number of kneecaps you have. (106)

Add the digits together. (7)

Subtract the greater number: 0.08 or 0.8. (6.2)

Whisper your answer to your neighbor. (6.2)

Math Concepts: division, addition, subtraction, number sequence, decimals

6.2

Mental Math • 5–6 © 2001 Creative Teaching Press

MENTAL MATH 107

Start with the mode of 12, 106, 5, and 106. (106)

Add the digits together. (7)

Multiply that number by 2^3. (56)

Multiply the digit in the ones place by the digit in the tens place. (30)

Whisper your answer to your neighbor. (30)

Math Concepts: vocabulary, addition, multiplication, place value

30

MENTAL MATH 108

Start with the range of 1,000; 1,500; and 2,000. (1,000)

Divide that number by 10^2. (10)

Multiply that number by 0.009. (0.09)

Double that number. (0.18)

Round that number to the nearest tenth. (0.2)

Whisper your answer to your neighbor. (0.2)

Math Concepts: vocabulary, division, multiplication, decimals, rounding numbers

0.2

MENTAL MATH
109

Start with the number of days in one week. (7)

Square that number. (49)

Round that number to the nearest ten. (50)

Add 7.7 to that number. (57.7)

Subtract the greater number: 0.03 or 0.3. (57.4)

Add the digits together. (16)

Show me the digit in the ones place with your fingers. (6)

Math Concepts: calendar, multiplication, rounding numbers, addition, decimals, subtraction, number sequence, place value

Mental Math • 5–6 © 2001 Creative Teaching Press

MENTAL MATH
110

Start with the number of shoes in one pair. (2)

Add 7^2. (51)

Subtract the multiple of 8: 26, 32, or 41. (19)

Round that number to the nearest ten. (20)

Whisper your answer to your neighbor. (20)

Math Concepts: addition, multiplication, subtraction, vocabulary, rounding numbers

20

Mental Math • 5–6 © 2001 Creative Teaching Press